To:

....

From:

....

West Side Publishing is a division of Publications International, Ltd.

Louis Weber, CEO
Publications International, Ltd.
7373 North Cicero Avenue
Lincolnwood, Illinois 60712

ISBN-13: 978-1-4127-1582-9
ISBN-10: 1-4127-1582-2

Manufactured in China.

8 7 6 5 4 3 2 1

Kids Say the Cutest Things About
God

Illustrations by Amanda Haley

WEST
SIDE
PUBLISHING

God's pets are mostly goldfish. My brother has sent a lot up there!

Lily, age 11

One time God was in my room, and he just started shaking his head.

Jen, age 10

God wants kids to be quiet
in church so we don't wake
up all the sleeping people.

Keisha, age 7

When I was learning how to ride my bike, God helped me after my Dad let go.

Evan, age 6

God doesn't mind if I do a
not-so-nice thing if I say
I'm sorry to him at night.

Justin, age 7

When you say your
prayers, sometimes
you should ask God
how he's doing.

Bailey, age 9

Dear God: How come you didn't make more modern stuff in the olden days?

Claire, age 10

God eats bread and fishes—the stuff he makes for everyone else.

Maria, age 8

God made the dinosaurs,
but they didn't work out.

Will, age 9

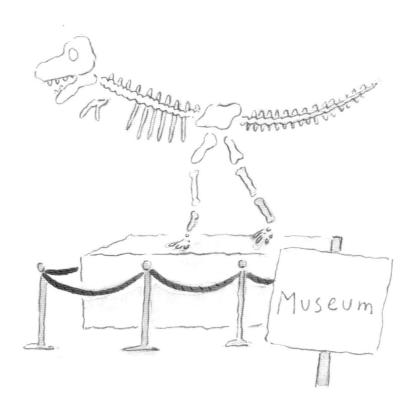

God is the same age as my great-grandpa—about a hundred.

Max, age 7

If God makes everything, like the sun and trees and lakes, why can't he make my bed?

Arun, age 10

God gave me my Mom and
not some other lady because
my Mom looks like me.

Chessa, age 6

God must not weigh
very much, because he
can walk on water and
clouds and he doesn't
fall through.

Tricia, age 10

One time when I saw a rainbow,
God was finger painting.

Gideon, age 6

God must have seen
me the other day,
so that's how come
I got grounded.

Adam, age 9

Yes, God gets tired. Like the time he sent me my brother instead of the puppy I asked him for.

Lucy, age 8

Dear God: Could you do a better job of putting people together? I fell out of a tree, and my arm broke just like that!

Sean, age 9

When God needs quiet time,
he just makes us sleepy.

Rhianna, age 7

When God can't answer a prayer, he looks it up in the Bible.

David, age 11

God only eats food
that the angels make
for him. My Mom makes
their cake sometimes.

George, age 8

Our minister does all
the talking, and God
does all the listening.

Tonya, age 11

The best thing God made
was Saturdays.

Nate, age 7

God uses prayers to find
people who need something.

Kenny, age 10

God created
Moms and Dads
because he can't
be two places at
the same time.

Nico, age 8

God doesn't have wings,
so he walks around
heaven. When he gets tired,
angels carry him.

Gina, age 7

God helps babies,
'cause they can't
hardly do anything.

Reece, age 9

God makes Santa listen
to some prayers, too.

Shana, age 5

God walks around
heaven with his
guarding angels
around him.

Jack, age 10

God likes all kinds
of food—but
not devil eggs.

Erica, age 8

God mostly wears long robes, 'cause he doesn't much like suits and ties.

Sara, age 7

When God gets done
creating things, he gets to
watch one hour of TV.

Cole, age 9

God sleeps right on the clouds,
but the angels need beds or
they fall through.

Maddie, age 7

I like Sunday school
because God
doesn't give us any
math to do.

Shane, age 9

God laughs all
the time, but
you wouldn't
know it from
his pictures!

Anna, age 10

God never gets
any older, and he
doesn't take a
bad picture.

Noah, age 9

God leaves the sun on
longer in the summer
so we can play more.

Nikki, age 8

God shakes snow out
of the clouds so we
can go sledding.

Carlos, age 7

Amanda Haley graduated from The School of the Art Institute of Chicago with a BFA in painting and drawing. She has illustrated more than 40 children's books, including both fictional and educational titles. Haley lives in Virginia with her husband, Brian, and dog, Mayzie.

Publications International, Ltd., wishes to thank the following schools for their submissions to *Kids Say the Cutest Things About God*:
Brennermann School (Chicago, IL), Bush Elementary School (Fulton, MO), Conn-West Elementary School (Grandview, MO), Gilkey Elementary School (Plainwell, MI), Holy Family School (Granite City, IL), Kennedy Middle School (Kankakee, IL), King Lab Magnet School (Evanston, IL), Plantation Park Elementary School (Plantation, FL), St. Agatha Catholic Academy (Chicago, IL), Starr Elementary School (Plainwell, MI)